SHEPHERD'S PIE

A Comedy for Women
in One Act

by

MABEL CONSTANDUROS
and HOWARD AGG

SAMUEL   FRENCH

LONDON
NEW YORK TORONTO SYDNEY HOLLYWOOD

Copyright © 1940 by Samuel French Ltd
All Rights Reserved

SHEPHERD'S PIE is fully protected under the copyright laws of the British Commonwealth, including Canada, the United States of America, and all other countries of the Copyright Union. All rights, including professional and amateur stage productions, recitation, lecturing, public reading, motion picture, radio broadcasting, television and the rights of translation into foreign languages are strictly reserved.

ISBN 978-0-573-03305-6

www.samuelfrench.co.uk
www.samuelfrench.com

For Amateur Production Enquiries

United Kingdom and World
excluding north america
plays@samuelfrench.co.uk
020 7255 4302/01

Each title is subject to availability from Samuel French,
depending upon country of performance.

CAUTION: Professional and amateur producers are hereby warned that SHEPHERD'S PIE is subject to a licensing fee. Publication of this play does not imply availability for performance. Both amateurs and professionals considering a production are strongly advised to apply to the appropriate agent before starting rehearsals, advertising, or booking a theatre. A licensing fee must be paid whether the title is presented for charity or gain and whether or not admission is charged.

The Professional Rights in this play are controlled by Samuel French Ltd, 24-32 Stephenson Way, London NW1 2HD.

No one shall make any changes in this title for the purpose of production. No part of this book may be reproduced, stored in a retrieval system, or transmitted in any form, by any means, now known or yet to be invented, including mechanical, electronic, photocopying, recording, videotaping, or otherwise, without the prior written permission of the publisher. No one shall upload this title, or part of this title, to any social media websites.

The right of Mabel Constanduros and Howard Agg to be identified as authors of this work has been asserted in accordance with Section 77 of the Copyright, Designs and Patents Act 1988.

CHARACTERS

(Who also appear in "Goose Chase")

GREAT AUNT POPSY.
LIZZIE FOGDEN (her Niece).
JANE FOGDEN
PEGGY FOGDEN } (LIZZIE's Daughters).
MISS IGGULDEN (a Busybody).
COWSLIP (a Dairymaid).
JUNE HOLLAND (a Neighbour).
THE VISITOR.

SHEPHERD'S PIE

The SCENE *is the living-room at the Fogdens' Farm on a summer afternoon.*

It is a pleasant, sunny room and the old pieces of furniture give it a warm and friendly look. A door up L. *leads to the rest of the house. A leaded, chintz-curtained window is in the* L. *wall. The fireplace is* R., *with an oak shelf above it.*

Above the fireplace is an old horsehair armchair, rather dilapidated and facing down stage. There is a dresser back C., *with the family tea service arranged on the shelves. A round table slightly* R. *of* C. *A sofa, set at an angle* L. *of* C. *There are two chairs at the table, and a small low one down* L.

(*See the Ground Plan.*)

When the CURTAIN *rises,* GREAT AUNT POPSY *is sitting in the armchair, as usual. She is an implacable old lady of over eighty, with a shawl round her shoulders and a lace cap on her head. At the moment she is bent almost double over a newspaper, spread on her lap, which she is reading avidly with the help of a hand reading-glass.* JANE FOGDEN, *a nice-looking country girl of about twenty, has just placed a bowl of summer flowers on the table, and is standing back admiring them when her mother,* LIZZIE FOGDEN, *bustles in up* L., *taking off her apron as she enters. She is a kind, homely-looking, business-like woman of about forty-five.*

JANE. Don't they look nice, Aunt Pops?
AUNT POPSY (*looking up for a second only*). 'Orrible!
JANE. Oh, Aunt Pops, I think they're lovely. (*Turning to her mother.*) Don't you, Mother?
LIZZIE (*abstractedly—putting her apron behind a sofa*

cushion). What ? Yes, very nice. But they'll drop all over the carpet, you know.

JANE. D'you think I ought to put some in her room ?

LIZZIE. I shouldn't. (*Crossing up* c., *to the dresser.*) They may give her hay-fever and then we shall have to carry all her meals up.

JANE (*carrying the flowers to the window table*). I've got out the rhubarb wine.

LIZZIE. Then you can put it away again. We'll begin as we mean to go on—with water.

AUNT POPSY (*looking up again and speaking with her mouth full of chewing-gum*). 'Orrible, that's wot it is. Blood-curdlin'. (*She goes on with her reading.*)

LIZZIE. What's the matter, Aunt Pops ? Jane, I do hope this woman isn't going to be faddy over her food. (*She goes round the room tidying things up.*)

JANE (*moving to* c., *and helping her*). Well, of course we don't know anything about her. Suppose she has peculiar pets. Like that woman who stayed at Cold Harbour and had rats running all over her while she ate her meals.

LIZZIE. Well, this Miss What's-It wrote on very nice notepaper.

JANE. So did the woman who stayed with Mrs. Bodger last summer—and *she* turned out to be a nudist. (*She picks up her knitting from the table.*)

LIZZIE. Well, whatever she is we've got to put up with her. Put that knitting away, Jane.

JANE (*as she stuffs it behind another sofa cushion*). I hate not having the house to ourselves.

LIZZIE (*still busy about the room*). Remember, she means four good guineas a week and she's staying here three months—*if* she's comfortable. So she's got to *be* comfortable, mind.

JANE (*sitting on the sofa*). I can't think what she wants to come to a place like this for. There are no shops, no cinema, no golf-course—nothing.

LIZZIE. I told her all that and she said it was charming.

JANE. Well, then she's mad. She must be.

LIZZIE (*crossing to the window* L.). Now stop it, Jane. What's the good of meeting trouble half-way? Put this book away, there's a good girl. (*She looks out of the window.*)

JANE (*rising and crossing up* C.). Well, she sounds peculiar to me—"Evadne Vaughan Farquharson." (*She puts the book in the dresser drawer.*)

LIZZIE (*moving to the head of the sofa*). She can't help the name she was born with.

JANE (*returning to below the sofa*). Well, if *I* was landed with a name like that I wouldn't rest until I'd done something about it—even if his name was Fish. (*She sits.*)

AUNT POPSY. Well, it wasn't. It was 'Arris.

LIZZIE (*crossing up* C.). Whose name was Harris?

AUNT POPSY. Come 'ome from the office 'e did, like a unsuspectin' lark, sits down to 'is tea, clashes 'is teeth into a innercent-lookin' shepherd's pie, and the next minute—bang!—'e falls down in a frothin' fit.

LIZZIE (*above and* L. *of the table*). Who does?

AUNT POPSY. Mr. 'Arris.

LIZZIE (*impatiently*). But who *is* Mr. Harris?

AUNT POPSY. 'E ain't anybody now. 'E's been murdered. 'Aven't you read the paper?

LIZZIE (*turning up to the dresser*). How can I when you sit on it all day? What's the time, Jane?

JANE (*looking at the clock on the mantelpiece*). Half-past twelve.

LIZZIE. Goodness, she'll soon be here. (*She comes down to the table with a cloth.*)

AUNT POPSY. Who will?

LIZZIE (*spreading the cloth*). The lady who's coming to stay with us.

AUNT POPSY. Wot lady?

LIZZIE (*to* JANE). I shall have to tell her. Well, Aunt Pops, we're having a paying guest.

AUNT POPSY. Why?
LIZZIE (bus. at the table). Because I've been sitting in a tin bath in front of the kitchen fire for twenty years and I'm tired of it.
AUNT POPSY. Wot d'you do it for, then?
LIZZIE. Because we haven't got a bathroom—not that that interests you—and this lady's going to pay for it. (She fetches cutlery, etc., from the dresser.)
AUNT POPSY. Interfering old parrot! Why can't she stay at 'ome? Traipsin' about buyin' bathrooms for them as don't want 'em.
LIZZIE (working down below the table). Now look here, Aunt Pops: you've got to watch your tongue while she's here. You've got to be civil to her and if anyone asks you who she is——
JANE (butting in). Miss Iggulden's sure to.
LIZZIE. You've to say she's a friend of ours from Potter's Bar who's come to stay with us for a few weeks. We don't want the village to know that she's a paying guest.
AUNT POPSY (immersed in her paper). Ooh! They say 'is legs was round 'is neck when they found 'im.
LIZZIE. Round whose neck?
AUNT POPSY. Mr. 'Arris's.

(LIZZIE exchanges a bewildered glance with JANE, then turns to AUNT POPSY.)

LIZZIE. Whose legs were round Mr. Harris's neck?
AUNT POPSY. Mr. 'Arris's.
LIZZIE. Oh, do be quiet about Mr. Harris's legs and listen to me.
AUNT POPSY. It says 'ere where 'is face was that 'orrid bottle colour—like your Uncle Sam's got when 'e'd been in " The George " of a night—and 'is eyes bugged out like chapel 'at-pegs . . .
LIZZIE. Oh, Aunt Pops, must you go on about that murder?
AUNT POPSY. 'Ow that woman could 'ave sat there and watched 'im squirm . . . And she's still

roamin' about the country waitin' to do someone else in.

JANE. I know, Aunt Pops, but we haven't time to talk about it now.

LIZZIE (*crossing up to the dresser for more things*). Take that gum away from her, Jane. It looks so common to keep chewing, especially when Miss—er—What's-It comes.

JANE (*rising*). Oh, do try to remember her name, Mother. (*She crosses to* AUNT POPSY.)

LIZZIE. Well, I can't. It's such a silly one—Vogan Far-Que-Harson.

JANE (*turning to* LIZZIE). It's pronounced Vaughan Farquharson, Mother.

LIZZIE. How can it be?

JANE. I don't know, but it is. (*She turns to* AUNT POPSY.)

LIZZIE. I shall just call her Miss Er.

AUNT POPSY (*as* JANE *is about to take a piece of chewing-gum from the arm of her chair*). No, you don't! I'm sticking to this. (*She pops it quickly in her mouth.*)

LIZZIE. I hope you won't. The last time the Vicar came, you couldn't open your mouth to speak to him.

JANE (*helping to set the table*). Well, we don't particularly *want* her to talk to-day, do we?

LIZZIE (L. *of the table*). No, but I hate to see an old lady sitting chewing. You never know where she'll stick it, either. I found a piece in the most extraordinary place the other day, Jane, I tell you.

(JANE *works up stage* R. *of the table.* COWSLIP *enters up* L., *and moves a little down* L.C. *She is a heavily built, lumpish girl with a dull expression and adenoids. She stands gawkishly, holding out a basket to* LIZZIE.)

Yes, Cowslip, what is it?

COWSLIP. Basket.

LIZZIE. Yes, I can see that. But what's in it?

COWSLIP. Eggs.

LIZZIE. Where from?
COWSLIP. Hens.
LIZZIE. I know that, you silly girl. But which hens?
COWSLIP. Ourn.
LIZZIE (*exasperatedly*). Of course they are. But are they from the near field or the farther one?
COWSLIP (*nodding*). Uh . . .
LIZZIE. Oh, why am I surrounded by fools? All right, give them to me. I'll put them on the dresser. (*She takes the basket from* COWSLIP *and puts it on the dresser.*) And don't forget to call at the butcher's. He promised me some chops for to-night.

(JANE *works down below the table.*)

COWSLIP. I've been.
LIZZIE. Oh, good.
COWSLIP. No, it isn't.
LIZZIE. What?
COWSLIP. 'E's sold 'em all.
LIZZIE. Oh, that *is* too bad of him. What did you bring instead?
COWSLIP (*gaping*). Eh?
LIZZIE. You got something else, of course.
COWSLIP (*shaking her head*). No, you didn't tell me anything else, only chops, and 'e 'adn't any chops, so I couldn't bring 'em.
LIZZIE. Well, what are we to give Miss—er—What's-It for dinner to-night?
COWSLIP. There's some cold rabbit pie.
LIZZIE. Don't be silly. How can we give a London lady cold rabbit pie on her first evening? You'll have to go back and see what the butcher *has* got, Cowslip. Hurry up.
COWSLIP. It's no good.
LIZZIE. Why not?
COWSLIP. 'E's shut.
LIZZIE. Oh, how infuriating. Well, I'll tell you what—— (*She breaks off as an old, cracked bell tinkles in the house.*) Oh, lord, who's that?

(JANE *runs to the window.*)

COWSLIP. Can't see.
JANE (*looking out*). Oh, my goodness!
LIZZIE. What's the matter? Don't say it's Miss Er and she's got no clothes on?
JANE. It isn't her at all. It's Miss Iggulden.
LIZZIE. It would be. That woman's got a sixth sense that tells her when she isn't wanted.
JANE (*coming away from the window*). Well, the quicker we let her in, the quicker we'll get her out. Go and open the door, Cowslip.

(COWSLIP *pauses a moment, then slouches out of the room.*)

LIZZIE. Jane, she's got wind of something.
JANE. She can't have. We've not said a word to anyone.
LIZZIE. Now, Aunt Pops, if you tell Miss Iggulden who Miss What's-It really is, I'll give all your chewing-gum to the pigs.
AUNT POPSY (*still reading*). Well, I 'ope they 'ang 'er, that's all.
LIZZIE (*startled*). What?
JANE (*crossing* R., *below the table*). It's all right, Mother. She's still with Mr. Harris on the hearth-rug. She doesn't hear a word you say. (*She moves up* R. *of the table.*)
COWSLIP (*coming back and standing stupidly just inside the room*). 'Ere you are. It's Miss Iggulden.

(MISS IGGULDEN *comes in and* COWSLIP *goes out, shutting the door behind her.* MISS IGGULDEN *is a desiccated, twittering spinster of about sixty, in an old coat and skirt and a hat overcrowded with flowers. She finishes every speech, especially the barbed ones, with a little snigger.*)

MISS IGGULDEN (*advancing mincingly to* LIZZIE—*her hand extended*). Oh, how do you do, Mrs. Fogden. Lovely weather, isn't it?

LIZZIE (*with exaggerated cordiality*). Good morning, Miss Iggulden. How nice to see you. You've come for your eggs, I suppose.

MISS IGGULDEN. Well, if you've got them ready . . . (*To down* L.C.) Oh, there's Aunt Popsy! How's Aunt Popsy this morning? Pretty well?

LIZZIE (*to* L. *of the table*). Yes, she's very well. Jane, give Miss Iggulden her eggs. We don't want to keep her waiting. Have you brought a basket, Miss Iggulden?

MISS IGGULDEN (*sitting in the low chair down* L.). There, isn't that just like me! I said to dear Mummie before I started, "Remind me to take a basket, Mummie," I said; but she was so busy with our little Pussikins (we're expecting a happy event, you know, and she seemed a little triste this morning). And what with one thing and another the basket went clean out of our heads. And that reminds me: I passed your Peggy in the trap.

LIZZIE (*flatly*). Did you?

(*She looks meaningly at* JANE *who is attending to the eggs.*)

MISS IGGULDEN. Yes, she looked as if she was going up to the station. Was she?

LIZZIE. Yes, she was. Jane, I think we can lend Miss Iggulden a basket.

MISS IGGULDEN. No, no, I wouldn't dream of it. I've been so naughty over your baskets as it is. D'you know I've got *three*. Was Peggy going to send off a parcel—or meeting someone?

LIZZIE. She's meeting someone. Jane, you'll find a paper bag in that drawer. (*She points to the dresser.*) Put half a dozen eggs in that for Miss Iggulden.

(JANE *finds the bag and packs the eggs.*)

MISS IGGULDEN. It's so kind of you. I don't know what dear Mummie would do without her **breakfast eggie.** Is it someone I know, you're **expecting?**

LIZZIE. No, just a friend. (*To below the table.*)
MISS IGGULDEN. Oh, how nice. From London, too. It *is* the London train Peggy is meeting, isn't it?
LIZZIE. Yes. Have you got the eggs, Jane?
JANE (*bringing the bag of eggs down* L.C.). Here they are, Miss Iggulden.
MISS IGGULDEN. Thank you, Jane. (*She holds the bag on her lap.*) Will your friend be—staying long?

(LIZZIE *and* JANE *exchange embarrassed glances.* JANE *moves up to the dresser.*)

LIZZIE. Oh, about three months, I think.
MISS IGGULDEN. Three months! She must be a very dear friend.
LIZZIE (*hovering round her at* L.C.). Well, we won't keep you, Miss Iggulden.
MISS IGGULDEN. Oh, I'm in no hurry. I wonder if I might beg a glass of water? It's so hot and your well water is so delicious. "Adam's Ale" Mummie calls it. She's so quaint.
JANE (*after a glance at the clock and her mother—quickly*). I'll fetch a glass.

(*She hurries out up* L.)

MISS IGGULDEN. I suppose you're all going to the Cookery Lecture this afternoon?
LIZZIE. No, I'm afraid not.
MISS IGGULDEN. Oh no, of course, with your cousin just arriving . . .
LIZZIE. She's no relation at all.
MISS IGGULDEN. There, how silly of me! I thought you said she was. Just a very old friend?
LIZZIE. Yes, quite.
MISS IGGULDEN. Ah, as Mummie always says: "There's no friend like an old friend." She has such a knack of hitting the nail on the head. An old school-fellow, perhaps?

Lizzie (*her cordiality beginning to wilt*). *No*, Miss Iggulden.

(Jane *re-enters with a glass of water.*)

Jane (*handing it to* Miss Iggulden). Here you are, Miss Iggulden.

Miss Iggulden. Thank you, Jane. As Mummie says, yours is a really Vintage water. (*She giggles and drinks.*)

Lizzie. Well, Miss Iggulden, I expect it's nearly your lunchtime.

Miss Iggulden. Well, as a matter of fact, Mummie and I looked at each other this morning and said: "Lunch? No!" We simply couldn't face it in this heat. So I've absolutely nothing to do till I go to the Lecture at three—and this is really on my way.

(Lizzie *and* Jane *look at each other in agony.*)

If you don't mind putting up with me.... (*She takes another sip.*) Delicious!

Jane (*a note of alarm in her voice*). Here's Peggy with the trap, Mother.

Miss Iggulden. Oh, your visitor. Don't take any notice of me, will you? Just carry on with your lunch and I shall be as happy as a squirrel, sitting here with my lovely drink. (*She sips with gusto.*)

Lizzie. Excuse me, Miss Iggulden, I must just go and see to things.

Miss Iggulden. Yes, of course, dear. I'm not here really. I'm just a little wraith in the corner.

Lizzie (*under her breath*). I wish you were. Come along, Jane...

(*They both go out.* Miss Iggulden *goes to the window and looks out.*)

Aunt Popsy (*fixing* Miss Iggulden *with a baleful eye*). D'you think they'll catch 'er?

SHEPHERD'S PIE

Miss Iggulden (*starting*). What ? Well, she's here.

Aunt Popsy (*alarmed*). Where ?

Miss Iggulden. Just getting out of the trap.

Aunt Popsy. 'Orrors!

Miss Iggulden (*at once sensing something and moving to* R.C., *below the table*). Oh. Oh, you don't like her, then ?

Aunt Popsy. Like 'er ? Who could ?

Miss Iggulden (*warming*). I see. Isn't she—a—*nice* woman ?

Aunt Popsy. Nice ? She's a fiend in 'uman clothin'.

Miss Iggulden. Oh dear. Isn't it going to be rather unpleasant having her here ?

Aunt Popsy (*frightened*). Unpleasant ? It's puttin' our 'eads in the tiger's mouth. What she's done once, she'll do again.

Miss Iggulden (*feeling she is on the brink of big things*). Really ? I'd no idea I'd stumbled across a family . . . well . . . It's most awkward. I mean, she'll be here in a minute. . . . (*She turns to* C., *glancing at the window.*)

Aunt Popsy. Then you'd better ring up the Police. Quick !

Miss Iggulden (*turning towards* Aunt Popsy). Police ! Did you say the Police ?

Aunt Popsy. I did. Ring 'em up.

Miss Iggulden. But good gracious, you don't mean to say that she's—wanted ?

Aunt Popsy. Well, of course they want 'er.

Miss Iggulden. Oh dear, this is terrible ! Does Mrs. Fogden know ?

Aunt Popsy. Well, I've been reading out about it all the morning, but she don't listen.

Miss Iggulden. You mean—she's mentioned in the paper ?

Aunt Popsy. All over 'em. 'Ave a bit of gum ? (*She unsticks a piece from the chair leg and holds it out to* Miss Iggulden.)

Miss Iggulden (*in horror*). No, no, thank you. I couldn't possibly. I'm really too upset.

Aunt Popsy. I 'ope she don't struggle when they take 'er, that's all. It turns me to see anyone writhin'.

Miss Iggulden (*mopping her brow*). Oh dear!

Aunt Popsy. Not that a bit of writhin' wouldn't do 'er good—on the 'earth-rug too. Like 'er poor victim.

Miss Iggulden (*horrified*). Victim! You don't mean that she's——?

Aunt Popsy. Yes. Shepherd's pie, that's 'er line.

Miss Iggulden. Shepherd's pie?

Aunt Popsy. Yes, incinerated 'erself into 'is house, give 'im a nice tasty bit for 'is tea, and 'e'd 'ardly time to crumple up on the 'earth-rug before 'e was gone.

Miss Iggulden (*in a wailing voice*). A poisoner! A poisoner!

Aunt Popsy (*ghoulishly*). Yes. 'Ere, read about 'er. (*She holds out the paper.*)

Miss Iggulden. No, no, I couldn't! (*In great agitation.*) But why are you shielding her? I mean she ought to be handed over to justice.

Aunt Popsy. Lizzie wants her money for a bathroom.

Miss Iggulden (*appalled*). But I never heard of anything so sordid. I couldn't set foot in a bath that had been paid for in—well—blood.

Aunt Popsy. No more wouldn't I. I don't believe in settin' foot in 'em anyway—nasty wet things.

Miss Iggulden. Oh dear, they're coming. I can hear them. (*Crossing down* L.) One's at such a disadvantage . . . I mean I've never met a—one doesn't know how to behave. . . .

(*The door opens and* Lizzie *comes in, followed by the* Visitor.)

Lizzie. And this is our living-room . . .

SHEPHERD'S PIE

(MISS IGGULDEN *recoils against the wall down* L., *with her eyes popping out in horror.*)

AUNT POPSY (*muttering*). It won't be long. It'll be a morgue.

(*The* VISITOR *is a forthright, tweed-clad spinster of about forty, with dark glasses and carrying an attaché case.*)

VISITOR (*looking round the room*). Very nice.

LIZZIE. And this is my husband's aunt. Everyone calls her Aunt Pops. She's eighty-four, aren't you, Aunt Pops?

AUNT POPSY (*truculently*). Yes, but I ain't done with life yet.

VISITOR (*to her—heartily*). No, I'm sure you haven't. I should think it would take a lot to kill you.

(MISS IGGULDEN *shrinks further into the wall and emits a groan, stifling it with her hand.*)

LIZZIE (*suddenly remembering her*). Miss Iggulden, aren't you well?

MISS IGGULDEN (*now thoroughly demoralized—in a long-drawn-out wail*). Noooo!

VISITOR (*coming over to her—briskly*). I expect it's the heat. I think I can give you something for that. (*She begins to open her attaché case on the sofa.*)

MISS IGGULDEN (*terrified and gasping*). No, no, thank you, really. I'd rather not. Really I would. I'm quite all right.

VISITOR. Just as you like. Oh, here's a little present for you. (*She hands a round paper parcel to* LIZZIE, *which she has taken from her case.*) I always bring something for my hostess on these occasions.

LIZZIE. Thank you very much.

VISITOR. I made it myself, so I know it's nice.

LIZZIE. It's very good of you. (*She puts the parcel down on the table.*)

VISITOR. Not at all. It's very good of you to have me. (*She moves to the sofa.*)

LIZZIE. Would you like to see your room?

VISITOR (*turning, a little surprised*). Well, I—yes, that *is* kind of you. I really should like a little rest before lunch. Just to collect my thoughts, you know.

LIZZIE. Of course. I'll get my daughter to take you up. (*She goes over to the door and calls.*) Peg-gy! (*She returns to above the table.*)

VISITOR (*sitting on the sofa*). What a charming old place. It's so restful. I've had to rush about such a lot lately.

AUNT POPSY. I expect you have.

VISITOR. Yes, I seem to be wanted here, there and everywhere. There's no rest for the wicked, is there?

(MISS IGGULDEN *lets out another wail.*)

(*Turning kindly to her.*) I'm afraid you're still feeling unwell. I wish you'd let me give you something.

MISS IGGULDEN (*almost choking*). No, no, thank you.

(PEGGY *enters up* L. *She is* JANE'S *younger sister, a pretty girl of about sixteen.*)

PEGGY (*to* L.C.). Did you call me, Mother?

LIZZIE. Yes, dear. (*She continues setting the table.*) Will you take Miss—er—up to her room?

VISITOR (*rising*). Thank you so much. (*She picks up her attaché case.*)

PEGGY (*as they move to the door*). I'm afraid the stairs are rather slippery. I'm sure someone'll break their neck on them one day.

VISITOR (*as they go out*). Oh, well, I always say that you'll die when your time comes and not before. . . .

AUNT POPSY (*when the door has shut*). Well, *she* ought to know if anyone does.

LIZZIE. What do you mean, Aunt Pops?

MISS IGGULDEN (*moving in a pace or two, distressed,*

and in great agitation). Oh, Mrs. Fogden, please, please, I beg of you, don't go on with this.

LIZZIE (*taking a pace towards her*). Don't go on with what, Miss Iggulden?

MISS IGGULDEN. Even if she is an old friend. I mean if you want a bathroom so badly, I'll get up a subscription in the village . . . I'll do anything . . .

LIZZIE (*turning and glaring at* AUNT POPSY). I see. Aunt Pops has told you.

MISS IGGULDEN. Yes. (*Clasping her hands—distractedly.*) Oh, Mrs. Fogden, think of the—the blood.

LIZZIE. What blood?

MISS IGGULDEN. On her head.

LIZZIE. Miss Iggulden, the sun *has* upset you. I think you ought to lie down.

AUNT POPSY. Yes, put 'er on the 'earth-rug. It'll save 'er movin'.

(JANE *enters up* L. MISS IGGULDEN *moves down* L., *and turns.*)

JANE (*to the head of the sofa*). Mother, it's rather funny, she hasn't brought any luggage.

AUNT POPSY. She won't need any. If she 'ad, it'd be took away from 'er.

LIZZIE. Who by?

AUNT POPSY. The Police. Lizzie, why didn't you tell me who she was?

LIZZIE. But I did.

AUNT POPSY. You told me she was a paying guest from Someone's Bar. According to Miss Iggulden she's the woman wot done in Mr. 'Arris.

(LIZZIE *and* JANE *look at* MISS IGGULDEN.)

MISS IGGULDEN (*sitting down* L.). How can you say that? It was *you* who told *me*.

(*They look at* AUNT POPSY.)

AUNT POPSY. You story! I was speaking of the murder and I asked you if you thought they'd catch 'er and you said she was outside and then in she walked.

LIZZIE (*turning to her*). Miss Iggulden, how could you *say* such a thing?

MISS IGGULDEN. I'm terribly sorry. I misunderstood Aunt Pops. We were talking at cross-purposes. I thought from what she said that this lady was—well—a notorious character.

LIZZIE (*firmly*). Nothing of the sort. She's a Miss —what's her name, Jane?

JANE. Vaughan Farquharson, Mother.

LIZZIE. She's unmarried, she's come here as a paying guest and she lives at Potter's Bar. Now are you satisfied?

MISS IGGULDEN. Well, of course, Mrs. Fogden. If only you'd told me this in the first instance . . .

LIZZIE. If you hadn't been the biggest gossip in the village, I might have.

MISS IGGULDEN (*rising—outraged*). MRS. FOGDEN!!

LIZZIE. Well, you know you are. You came here this morning purposely to find out who was coming to stay.

MISS IGGULDEN. Indeed I had no such thought.

LIZZIE. Yes, you had. (*Her voice begins to quaver.*) And now you'll just delight in telling everyone that we've had to take in a paying guest because we want a bathroom. (*Sitting* L. *of the table.*) I wish she *had* been a murderess. (*She sniffs into her handkerchief.*)

JANE (*putting her hand on her shoulder*). Now, don't upset yourself, Mother.

MISS IGGULDEN (*sniffing into her handkerchief*). What about me? (*Sitting on the sofa.*) I come here in the most harmless manner for a few simple eggs and first I'm terrified nearly to death by murderesses and then I'm insulted. (*She bursts into tears.*)

JANE (*going to her*). Oh, Miss Iggulden, do stop. It was only Aunt Pops's nonsense.

AUNT POPSY. That's right. Blame it on me—all the lot of you. 'Ow was I to know Miss Iggulden was

tellin' a pack of lies? (*She begins to grow tearful.*) Deceivin' a poor old woman of eighty-four.
  JANE (*crossing* R.). Now don't *you* start, Aunt Pops. Here you are. Here's your gum. (*She pops a piece in her mouth.*) Now suck that and be quiet. (*She turns to* R. *of the table.*)

(PEGGY *re-enters up* L.)

  PEGGY. I say, isn't she nice? She takes such an interest in everything. She made me show her the kitchen on the way up.
  LIZZIE (*suddenly remembering—jumping up*). Lunch! Potatoes! They ought to go on at once. (*Stiffly.*) Ask Miss Iggulden if she'll be staying for lunch, Jane. (*She turns up to the dresser.*)
  MISS IGGULDEN (*rising—with hauteur*). Tell your mother, Jane, that I'd rather die.

(MISS IGGULDEN *gathers herself together prepared to sweep out, but* COWSLIP *is already in the doorway.*)

  COWSLIP. Oh—er——
  LIZZIE (*above and* L. *of the table*). Yes, what is it?
  COWSLIP. I don't know. I 'aven't opened it.
  LIZZIE. Opened what?
  COWSLIP. This. (*She holds out a dirty, crumpled telegram which she has taken from her pocket.*)
  LIZZIE (*taking it from her*). A telegram. When did this come?
  COWSLIP. Yesterday.
  LIZZIE. Yesterday? And you've had it all this time!
  COWSLIP. No. I dropped it in the cowshed. Wonder Clover 'adn't ate it.
  JANE. It looks as though she'd tried.
  LIZZIE. You stupid girl. People don't send telegrams for nothing. It may be something most important.
  JANE. Yes, it may. Hadn't you better open it, Mother?
  LIZZIE (*tearing it open and then holding it at arm's*

length). I can't see it without my glasses. Oh, read it, Peggy.

(PEGGY *crosses to* LIZZIE *and takes the telegram.*)

PEGGY (*reading*). "So sorry. Unable to travel to-morrow. Please meet same train Friday."

LIZZIE. Well, whoever can that be from?

PEGGY. It's signed "Vaughan Farquharson."

LIZZIE. Who's that? Oh yes, of course.

JANE. But Miss Vaughan Farquharson has come. She's here.

PEGGY. But she can't be. It's only Thursday to-day and she distinctly says in the telegram that she won't be coming till Friday.

JANE. Good lord! Then this can't be her!

LIZZIE. Who can't be whom?

JANE. Miss Vaughan Farquharson. She isn't here at all.

LIZZIE. Isn't here! Then *who* is the woman upstairs?

MISS IGGULDEN (*whose eyes have been going eagerly from one to the other—waspishly*). Yes, who indeed?

COWSLIP. Can I go?

LIZZIE. Yes, as far away as possible.

COWSLIP. Ta, then I'll go to the pictures.

(*She slops out.*)

MISS IGGULDEN. Yes, I wonder who it is you've got in your house, Mrs. Fogden? An impostor, evidently.

LIZZIE (*to* PEGGY). What happened when you met her at the station, Peggy?

PEGGY. Well, she was the only stranger who got out of the train, so I went up to her and said: "Are you the lady I've come to meet?" and she said: "Yes, if your mother is my kind hostess"—and you are—so I brought her.

JANE (*moving to below the table*). But didn't you ask her if her name was Vaughan Farquharson?

PEGGY. No, she was the only one there so I thought she must be.

JANE. Well, of course, I concluded she was, so I've never called her by her name.

LIZZIE. I can't remember it, anyhow, so I've called her Miss Er all the time. I said I should. (*She sits* L. *of the table, her back to* MISS IGGULDEN.)

MISS IGGULDEN. Well, this seems to me a very peculiar situation. Here you have a woman upstairs in your spare room and you don't know in the least who she is.

LIZZIE. Tell Miss Iggulden, Jane, that I'm quite aware of that.

JANE. But I don't understand it. Why has she come here ?

PEGGY. How did she know we were expecting someone ?

JANE. I thought it was funny she didn't bring any luggage.

MISS IGGULDEN. Surely the sensible thing is for one of you to go up and ask her who she is.

LIZZIE. Tell Miss Iggulden, Jane, that we can't very well do that since apparently we've accepted her.

JANE. If only there was something that could give us a clue. (*Suddenly.*) Her coat . . .

PEGGY. She took it up with her.

MISS IGGULDEN. I know ! There's that parcel she gave Mrs. Fogden. Perhaps there's an address inside on the paper.

JANE. *Did* she give you a parcel, Mother ?

LIZZIE. Yes, it's there on the table.

PEGGY (*crossing to above the table*). Let's open it . . . my word, it's heavy. . . .

(*She begins to unwrap the parcel with* JANE *looking on and* MISS IGGULDEN *hovering excitedly about them.*)

MISS IGGULDEN. It's a dish of something.

PEGGY (*removing the wrapping*). It's a pie. A shepherd's pie, Mother.

(*She hands the dish to* LIZZIE, *who has risen.*)

LIZZIE (*taking the dish*). So it is. Looks a nice one, too.

JANE (*turning over the paper wrapping*). There's no name anywhere on the paper. There's still nothing to tell us who she is.

AUNT POPSY. What more do you want? Who poisoned Mr. 'Arris?

LIZZIE. Oh, I don't know and I don't care.

AUNT POPSY. Well, I'll tell you. Mrs. Barnes— 'is 'ousekeeper. And wot did she do it with? Shepherd's pie. And wot's in that dish?

MISS IGGULDEN. Mrs. Fogden, she's right! She's right! (*She sits on the sofa.*)

AUNT POPSY. Of course I am. Read wot it says 'ere . . . (*She holds out the paper which* JANE *takes from her.*)

JANE (*reading*). " Mrs. Barnes———"

AUNT POPSY (*pointing upwards with her thumb*). That's 'er real name.

JANE. " Mrs. Barnes is a well-spoken woman of about forty, respectably dressed and wearing glasses."

AUNT POPSY. Glasses! There you are.

JANE. " It is thought that she may try to evade capture by entering some household in the capacity of housekeeper or even paying guest. Anyone coming in contact with a suspicious character is advised to get in touch with the police."

AUNT POPSY. Well, go on. Wot are you waitin' for?

LIZZIE. Don't be silly, Aunt Pops. We can't make accusations like that. D'you want us all sued for libel?

MISS IGGULDEN. But it all fits in so.

JANE (*giving the paper back to* AUNT POPSY). Well, it's certainly funny.

MISS IGGULDEN. Funny! What an inadequate word.

PEGGY. You don't really think that it's—Mrs. Barnes we've got upstairs, do you, Mother?

LIZZIE. No, of course not.

Miss Iggulden. Then, who is she?
Lizzie. Well, I—I haven't thought.
Miss Iggulden. Then isn't it time you began? Here's a strange woman who has walked into your house and passed herself off as somebody else. Would she do that if she'd nothing to hide?
Jane. She must have had some purpose in coming here.
Miss Iggulden. Yes, what is it, I'd like to know?
Lizzie. That's what we've got to find out.
Jane. Now let's think. . . . What reason could a woman have for doing a thing like this?
Aunt Popsy. Murder!
Lizzie. Oh, do be quiet, Aunt Pops.
Peggy (*suddenly*). She might have lost her memory.
Lizzie. Come to think of it, she *did* say she'd like to have a rest before lunch—" to collect her thoughts."
Jane. She may actually be mad. She may have escaped from an asylum.
Peggy. She didn't seem mad.
Jane. But they're very cunning and sometimes they're only mad on one subject.
Aunt Popsy. Shepherd's pie!
Lizzie (*starting*). Ssh! She's coming down.

(*They all glance nervously at the door.*)

Miss Iggulden (*rising, in a flutter*). Oh dear, what shall we do? (*She moves down* L.)
Aunt Popsy. Tie 'er in a chair till the Police come!
Jane. Now look here, we've got to try and find out, without being too obvious, who she is, where she's come from, and what she's here for.
Lizzie. Quick! Don't let her think we've been talking about her. Where's my darning . . . I'll be doing that. (*She crosses to the sofa and takes her darning from behind a cushion, sits down quickly and begins to work.*)
Jane. And I'll be counting the eggs. (*Crossing to* Miss Iggulden.) Miss Iggulden, you better let

me have yours, too, or I shan't have enough. (*She snatches the bag of eggs away from* MISS IGGULDEN *and takes them over to the dresser.*)

PEGGY. What shall I do?

LIZZIE. Sit down and try and look nonkalant.

(PEGGY *crosses to above the sofa.*)

MISS IGGULDEN (*crossing quickly to* L. *of the table*). Look, let's put a chair where the light'll fall on her and we can see whether she's telling us the truth. (*She hurriedly turns the chair* L. *of the table so that the light from the window falls on it.*)

(*The door opens and the* VISITOR *comes in.* MISS IGGULDEN *just has time to rush back to the sofa and sit* L. *of* LIZZIE. *She begins to sing, rather too loudly, to cover her nervousness.*)

VISITOR (*coming into the room—gaily*). Oh, what a lovely old house. I shall never tear myself away.

(*They all look startled but manage to grin.*)

LIZZIE. Do sit down, won't you?

MISS IGGULDEN (*explosively*). Here! (*She indicates the chair* L. *of the table.*)

(PEGGY *moves above the little chair down* L.)

VISITOR. Thank you. I like the look of that little chair in the corner. May I sit there?

(PEGGY *checks, behind the sofa. There is an awkward silence as the* VISITOR *crosses down* L. *and sits.*)

(*To* JANE, *who is carrying the eggs to* L. *of the table.*) Are those your own eggs? How lovely to have hens.

MISS IGGULDEN (*leaning forward and fixing her with a glassy stare*). You're not used to the country, then?

VISITOR. I love it, of course.

MISS IGGULDEN. But you—*live* in a town?

VISITOR. Yes, I have to, because of my work.

PEGGY (*quickly and rather crudely*). Do you find that your—work makes you—very tired, so that your mind's apt to wander?

VISITOR (*smiling at her*). No. Why? Do I seem very absent-minded?
PEGGY (*in confusion*). Oh no, no. I just wondered, that's all. (*She moves away to the head of the sofa.*)

(LIZZIE *looks at her and she knows that she has failed. A pause.*)

JANE. I suppose you have a lovely flat all to yourself, have you?
VISITOR. No, I wish I had. I live with a lot of other women.
JANE (*with a look at* PEGGY). Oh, I see.
PEGGY. And you don't like it?
VISITOR. No. Sometimes they get on my nerves so, I feel I could poison them.
MISS IGGULDEN (*before she can stop herself, almost barking*). Oh!——
VISITOR. Still, of course, one does manage to give them the slip every now and then.

(*There is a blank pause. They all look frightened now. She evidently has escaped from a lunatic asylum.*)

PEGGY (*faltering*). The slip?
JANE (*nervously*). But—do you find that's worth it? I mean—you have to go back—don't you?
VISITOR. Oh, of course I grumble, but I really love my life.
LIZZIE (*thinking this over*). Do you?
VISITOR. Do you mind if I smoke?
LIZZIE. Oh, do. Give Miss—Er—a match, Peggy.

(JANE *hands* PEGGY *matches from the dresser. While the* VISITOR *gets out a cigarette,* PEGGY *strikes a match and holds it at arm's length as though terrified to go too near her.*)

VISITOR. Thank you.

(PEGGY *returns to the head of the sofa.* JANE *sits* L. *of the table. They all look desperately at one another, not knowing what to say next.*)

(*After an awkward pause.*) I see you've opened my little present.

LIZZIE (*awkwardly*). Yes, thank you.

(PEGGY *moves to above the table.*)

VISITOR. I do rather pride myself on my shepherd's pie.

MISS IGGULDEN (*humouring her*). It's *so* clever of you to make it.

VISITOR. Oh, it's quite easy when you've done it once. I must say I've been very successful with it.

AUNT POPSY. Yes, we know you 'ave; but don't you feel funny when you make it?

VISITOR. Funny?

AUNT POPSY. Yes, to think of them that'll 'ave to eat it?

VISITOR (*laughing*). Well, I've never had any complaints so far.

AUNT POPSY. No, there wasn't time.

VISITOR (*humouring the old lady*). You must let me know what *you* think of it.

AUNT POPSY (*outraged*). Well! Of all the——

(*The door opens and* COWSLIP *comes in.*)

COWSLIP. 'Ere's Miss 'Olland now.

(JUNE HOLLAND *comes in, a well-bred-looking girl of about twenty, more sophisticated than* JANE *or* PEGGY. *She is wearing a nice summer frock and a gay hat.*)

JUNE (*to down* L.C.). Oh, Mrs. Fogden, I *am* so sorry to barge in on you like this, just at lunchtime.

LIZZIE (*getting up*). Don't mention it, Miss June.

JUNE. But the policeman in the village told me that he'd seen Peggy driving away from the station with a strange lady.

VISITOR. Yes, it was me.

JUNE. Then you must be Miss Clairmont?

VISITOR. That's right.

JUNE. I'm terribly sorry. I should have met you,

SHEPHERD'S PIE

but I had a puncture, and when I got to the station you were gone. D'you mind if I hurry her away, Mrs. Fogden?

LIZZIE (*rising, completely dazed*). N-no.

VISITOR (*rising, rather dazed herself*). Shouldn't 1 be here, then?

JUNE. No, you're lunching with us.

VISITOR (*crossing to* JUNE). Then I'm in the wrong house? (*Turning to* LIZZIE.) You poor people! You must have wondered who I was.

LIZZIE (*smiling feebly*). We did, rather.

(MISS IGGULDEN *rises slowly*.)

JUNE. Well, I'm afraid lunch is waiting. We've got a soufflé and the Vicar—and neither of them improve with keeping. Thank you so much, Mrs. Fogden.

LIZZIE (*faintly*). Not at all. Good-bye.

JUNE. Oh, not good-bye. You *are* coming this afternoon, aren't you?

LIZZIE. Where?

JUNE. To the Cookery Lecture in the Schoolroom —at three.

VISITOR. I do hope you will, because I shall be giving the recipe for that shepherd's pie you were all so interested in. (*Briskly and brightly*.) Good-bye.

(*She follows* JUNE *to the door and they both go out*.)

LIZZIE (*crossing, after a short pause, to below the table*). Aunt Pops, you made me feel perfectly dreadful. Let that be a lesson to you. Not to see a murderess in a perfectly harmless cookery lecturer.

AUNT POPSY. Didn't she murder Mr. 'Arris, then?

LIZZIE. No, she did not.

AUNT POPSY. Oh, well, we mustn't give up 'ope. Perhaps the woman wot's comin' to-morrow did.

She sits chewing, her jaws working and her eyes fixed placidly on space as—

The CURTAIN *falls*.

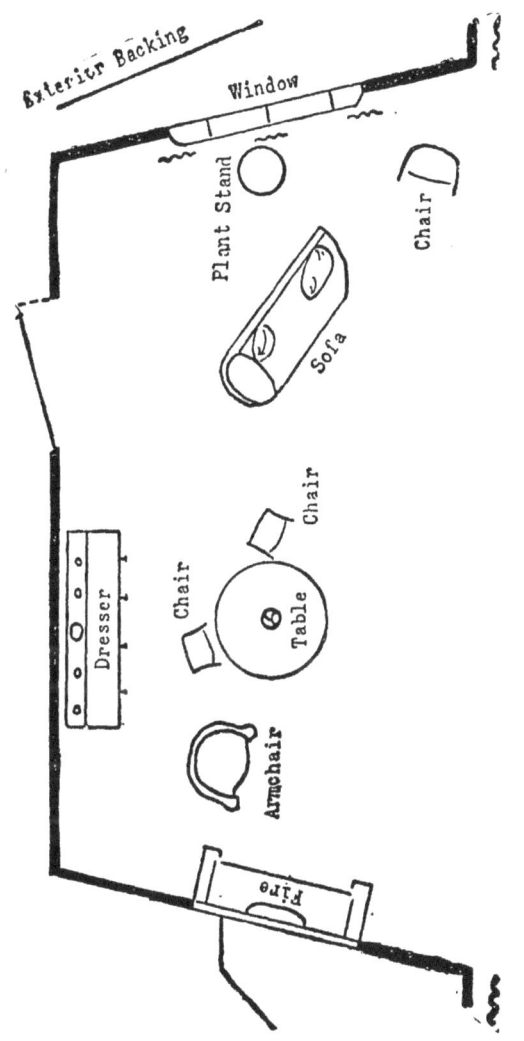

FURNITURE AND PROPERTY PLOT

Chintz curtains at window.

Carpet on stage.

Strip outside door.

1 old horsehair armchair (R.).

1 dresser (back C.).
   On it.—Family tea-service, etc.
     Matches.

In the Dresser Drawer.—Paper bags.
   Plush cloth.
   Cutlery, etc.

1 round table (R. of C.).
   On it.—Knitting.

2 small chairs (above and L. of table).

1 sofa, with two loose cushions.
   On the Sofa.—A book.
   Behind one cushion.—Darning.

1 small low chair (down L.).

1 small table or plant stand (at window).

On Mantel.—Clock.
   Ornaments.
   Mirror.

PERSONAL PROPERTIES.

Bowl of summer flowers (JANE *at rise of* CURTAIN).

AUNT POPSY.—Newspaper, chewing gum, hand reading-glass.

COWSLIP.—Basket of eggs, telegram in pocket.

VISITOR.—Attaché case containing a shepherd's pie in dish, wrapped in paper ; dark glasses.

Off L. (*for* JANE).—A glass of water.

LIGHTING PLOT

Floats.—Amber pink and white ½.

Battens.—Ditto, FULL.

Amber length on interior backing.

Straw flood outside windows, and to cover chair L. of the table.

No Cues.

Any character costumes or wigs needed in the performance of this play can be hired from Charles H. Fox Ltd, 184 High Holborn, London W C 1